Trader

Rebecca T. Tagoe

supported by
north west arts board

Text copyright © Rebecca T. Tagoe 1995
Illustrations, Jenny Bowers
Cover design, David Andrassy
Photographs, Patricia Duffin
Editor, Patricia Duffin

First published & distributed by Gatehouse Books Ltd in 1995
Reprinted 2000 by Gatehouse Books Ltd
Hulme Adult Education Centre, Stretford Road, Manchester M15 5FQ
Printed by RAP, 201 Spotland Road, Rochdale

ISBN 0 906253 46 2

British Library cataloguing in publication data:
A catalogue record for this book is available from the British Library

Our thanks for their ongoing support to Manchester Lifelong Learning.

Gatehouse gratefully acknowledges Barclays Age Resource Action Scheme for
financial assistance towards the production of this book. Gatehouse also owes
thanks to Manchester City Council and North West Arts Board for continued
financial support.

Thanks to the following groups from Manchester Adult Education Services for
piloting the early draft: Abraham Moss Centre, Greenheys Centre, Plant Hill
Centre.

Gatehouse is a member of The Federation of Worker Writers & Community
Publishers

Gatehouse provides an opportunity for writers to express their thoughts and
feelings on aspects of their lives.
The views expressed are not necessarily those of Gatehouse.

INTRODUCTION

I was born in Accra, Ghana.
I have lived in England for twenty years.
In England, I got a job
with the Education Authority,
as a cleaner in a school.
I enjoyed my job as a cleaner,
and also having fun with the kids.
Now I am retired, I miss my job.

I started classes four years ago,
to learn reading and writing.
I also did dressmaking and cookery.

Other people who have problems
with reading and writing
should come to classes.
It can help you, everywhere you go.

Rebecca T. Tagoe

When I was a young woman
in Ghana,
I was selling cloth
in the market in Accra.
I travelled to places far away
like Kumasi
to buy cloth.

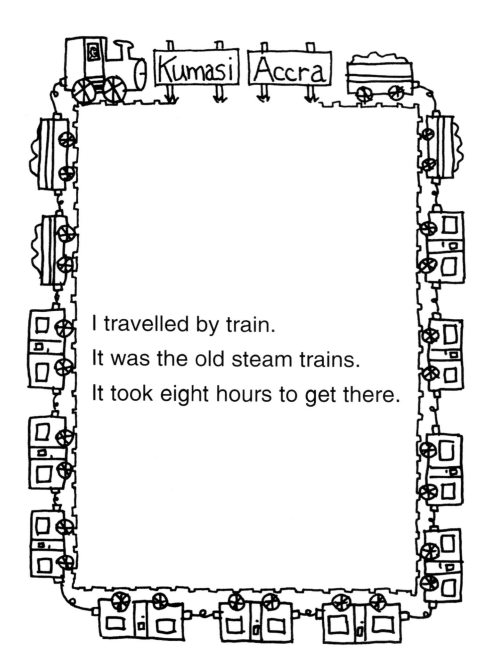

I travelled by train.

It was the old steam trains.

It took eight hours to get there.

6

When I was away,

my daughter

looked after the shop for me.

She did well.

I was happy as a trader,
buying the cloth.
People come from other countries
to buy cloth,
from Nigeria, Ivory coast,
Togo and the Hausa* people.
I met people
from many different countries.

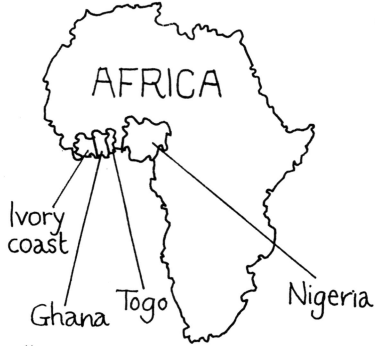

AFRICA

Ivory coast

Ghana   Togo   Nigeria

* say Howsa

8

I sold different kinds of cloth.

You have to make sure people like it
before you buy it.

You watch the materials that are liked
so you buy that material.

Adinkra cloth is popular
in many different countries.
It is made in Ghana,
in a big factory.
It is many different designs
and many colours,
and it is not too expensive.

Kente cloth
is very famous in Ghana
but it is very expensive,
because it takes a lot of work.
It is handmade.
Women can't make it. Men do it.
They do it in their own home,
in villages.

To be a trader
you have to have a pass book,
to buy cloth.
It is difficult to get the pass book,
but when you have it
you can go to different factories
to buy cloth.

In Ghana,

if you have some money,

you can be a trader or do anything.

Woman or man,

it doesn't matter.

When I came to Britain

I tried to continue this type of business.

It ended in disappointment.

I bought some goods

and asked somebody

to do the shipping for me.

Britain

Ghana

This person took money from me
to insure the goods.
Although he promised
to insure the goods
he did not do it.

When the ship carrying the goods
reached the West African coast
of Sierra Leone,
it caught fire and sank.
My goods were lost
and I couldn't claim any compensation
from anybody.
This has ruined my trade
up to the present day.

England is more difficult
for women to work.
In Ghana it is easier
to start a small business,
like mine.

HOW REBECCA WROTE HER STORY

Julie   We were reading a Gatehouse story
in our English group.
One person suggested
that we write our own story.
We agreed we'd all have a go.
I agreed to type them
and try to find someone to draw,
and make the stories into books.

Rebecca I chose to write about trading
because it was about Ghana
when I was young.
It was a happy time.
I told the story to Julie.

Julie   I wrote it down, it was quite short.
I asked lots of questions,
it turned into a conversation,
it was so interesting.

Rebecca When Julie asked questions,
I remembered more
and later
when Patricia asked questions
I remembered even more
and the story got longer.
I told the story.
Julie wrote it all down.
We read it back together
and changed things
if they weren't right.

Julie Everybody sent their stories
into Gatehouse
for the Beginner Reader competition.
It was Rebecca's story
that was chosen.

Rebecca T. Tagoe and Julie Northey
Hulme Adult Education Centre

Gatehouse Books

Gatehouse is a unique publisher

Our writers are adults who are developing their basic
reading and writing skills. Their ideas and experiences
make fascinating material for any reader, but are
particularly relevant for adults working on their reading
and writing skills. The writing strikes a chord - a shared
experience of struggling against many odds.

The format of our books is clear and uncluttered. The
language is familiar and the text is often line-broken, so
that each line ends at a natural pause.

Gatehouse books are both popular and respected within
Adult Basic Education throughout the English speaking
world. They are also a valuable resource within
secondary schools, Special Needs Education, Social
Services and within the Prison Education Service and
Probation Services.

Booklist Available

Gatehouse Books
Hulme Adult Education Centre
Stretford Road
Manchester M15 5FQ
Tel/Fax: 0161 226 7152
E-mail: office@gatehousebooks.org.uk
Website: www.gatehousebooks.org.uk

The Gatehouse Publishing Charity is a registered charity reg. no. 1011042
Gatehouse Books Ltd., is a company limited by guarantee, reg. no. 2619614